A Coventry Tale

Paul A M Palmer

Dedication

This book is dedicated to the City and people of Coventry for making me feel at home from the day that I first arrived.

CONTENTS

ACKNOWLEDGEMENTS

As ever, love and thanks go to Fliss as Editor-in-Chief and for listening to the many revisions of each work. I'm deeply indebted to my good friend Steve the illustrator who has done such a fine job in bringing the poems to life. Thanks also to Helen for the sanity check.

Special thanks also go to staff at the Reference Library in the Herbert Art Gallery in Coventry - leafing through a copy of the Leet Court book and viewing old photographs of Spicer Stoke Gate was an experience I shall never forget.

Finally, much love and thanks go to family and friends for their constant support and encouragement.

Introduction

A Coventry Tale is a work of fiction. It began with the writing of a poem on a medieval theme which brought the character of Odo to life. Ironically, that poem failed to make it into this collection, but the germ of the idea took hold and this book is the end result.

I have tried to ensure that the language is consistent with the 15th century - the only exception is *Beneath These Stones*, which is a retrospective poem at the end of the book. For example, I've used *mayhap* where we would today use *perhaps*, but I think this offers a more authentic feel to each speaker. Chaucer's *Canterbury Tales* has been a useful reference from a language perspective, but the age of some words has surprised me - *dizzy* has been around since the 1300s; for others I've used the original form - for example, *splendidious* was shortened to *splendid* at some stage in the English language. It has been an interesting experience to follow the words back to their roots, and Chaucer doesn't get all the plaudits!

The style of the poetry is intentionally contemporary in nature, so the poems and ballads *spoken* by the characters or *performed* by the minstrel in this book do not conform to those of the times. I have re-used and re-worked a couple of poems from my other collections because they seemed to fit with the mood and themes of the story.

There are plots that run through the book, but the intention is not to segment the stories as in the *Canterbury Tales*, so the characters simply interact as and when.

I am pleased to have such wonderful illustrations sitting alongside the words in this book and helping bring the words to life, thanks to the very fine talents of the artist.

I hope you enjoy reading *A Coventry Tale* and feel inspired to visit Coventry if you've never been before, or to follow one of the references listed in the *Author's Notes* section at the end of the book.

Historical Notes

The Leet Court

Coventry was ruled by its *Leet Court* from around 1425 until the dissolution of the monasteries. It elected the Mayor, picked the jury for every trial, and organised and ran the system of bailiffs. When the city wall was built, the *Leet Court* was responsible for ensuring that the *murage* (wall tax) was paid, so there is plenty of detail regarding its collection, as well as plenty of other useful research information in the *Leet Book* (translated and annotated by Mary Dormer Harris - see the *References* section at the end of the book).

The Gates

Coventry had twelve gates built, spaced out along the length of the wall when it surrounded the city. New Gate was the first to be constructed, guarding the approach from the London Road. By the year 1450, Dern Gate was known as Bastille Gate, but I have taken the liberty of sticking to the original name. They are listed below in a clockwise order (and appear in the illustrations as if on a clock face):

- Bishop Gate
- Cook Street Gate
- Priory Gate
- Dern Gate
- Gosford Gate
- New Gate
- Little Park Gate
- Cheylesmore Gate
- Greyfriars' Gate
- Spon Gate
- Hill Street Gate
- Well Street Gate

List of Characters

The characters in A Coventry Tale are a mixture of fictional and real. Firstly, the fictional characters:

Addy: Guardsman, romantically involved with Maud.

Ailwin (Hamo): Pilgrim visitor to Coventry, but disguised.

Bela: Maud's niece, lives and works in *The Star* inn.

Dizzy: Simpleton who begs for a living, pitied by everyone.

Eva: Weaver Masci's wife, lives in Spon St. - Odo's sister.

Fabian: Wealthy pilgrim, visiting St Osburga's tomb for his sick father.

Jocelin: Resident minstrel (troubadour) at *The Star* inn.

Masci: Weaver, Eva's husband.

Maud: Bela's Aunt and proud owner of *The Star* inn.

Odo: Eva's brother - the Prior's summoner, despised by all.

The following characters are taken from the *Leet Book* and other sources (see *Author's Notes* section):

John Arowe: Weaver.

Richard Austen: Capper (a cap-maker), member of the Leet Court.

Richard Botoner: a Mayor of Coventry, member of the Leet Court.

Richard Burnell: Goldsmith.

John De Colsale: Metalworker and bell-founder.

Will Crowe: Girdler (a belt-maker).

John Essex: a Mayor of Coventry, member of the Leet Court.

Thomas Hynkley: Mylner, (a seller of fancy goods - a *Milaner*).

Robert Stretton: Master Mason.

William Thomas: Weaver.

4

Narrator's Prologue

Welcome to this book of mine,
and take a step right back in time,

when Coventry had gates and wall,
the Leet Court ruling one and all.

Some characters may speak in rhyme
(not everywhere - most of the time!).

We'll lead you through this story bold
with artist's pictures to behold;

Some names are true and some are not -
sometimes we work with what we've got.

So please sit down, relax and read,
imagine that your drink is mead!

Apostles

Guardians of gold and silver,
of children and livestock,

of men and women,
of home and hostel,

of cloth and commerce,
of blue that's true,

of church and chapel,
of Priory and pilgrims.

We watch over the city
like twelve apostles,

walled up together, secure
in stone and mortar.

New Gate

I'm here to guard the London Road,
'tis why they built me first.

My brother gates came after me
and now we are well versed

in watching trade and travel flow
just like the Radford Brook.

Not many who come venture here
give us a second look!

Looking down the London Road
'tis pleasant in the sun,

and when the curfew bell has pealed
our work is never done.

If stars do hide and moon as well,
we stand here just the same,

unlike the torches burning bright,
we shall outlast the flame.

Narrator (Nightfall)

Now night has fallen, curfew's here,
but as you listen, please cup your ear:

the sound of laughter's in the air,
but others give a frightful scare.

There are smells of cooking in the pot,
for those that have or may have not;

bellies full or bellies empty,
for some are poor and some have plenty.

Now see what singing might be had,
within this city - good or bad!

A few short steps, 'tis not that far.
Jocelin's our man – he's at The Star.

Time And Tide

Jocelin sings:

The longest of waits at last is over!
Time and tide,
time and tide!

Our boat begins to rise and rise!
Time and tide,
time and tide!

Our charts are marked, the course is set.
Time and tide,
time and tide!

Our compass is shaking, the needle is nervous!
Time and tide,
time and tide!

At last, my love we swell and sway.
Time and tide,
time and tide!

Our vessel is rocking from side to side.
Time and tide,
time and tide!

But something is snagging or something is dragging!
Time and tide,
time and tide!

Our ship is still anchored, mayhap we are beached!
Time and tide,
time and tide.

We focus our love on the clear-blue sky.
Time and tide,
time and tide!

And the anchor's aweigh, the anchor's aweigh!
Time and tide,
time and tide!

Almost There

Fabian speaks:

On well-worn tracks with tired feet
we've travelled here in hope,
our company of souls all bound
by strands as taut as rope.

The Priory Gate looms large at last,
our journey's end in sight.
The Pilgrim's Rest is where we'll stay
in Palmer Lane this night.

There's one or two I'd care to lose
as we walk through these streets,
I've had enough of Hamo's ways
- see how he stabs his meat!

'Tis almost dusk, the curfew's close,
the guards have searched us hard.
We are the last of this day's throng,
with the heavy gates now barred.

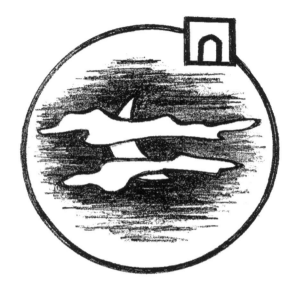

Priory Gate

Speaking of Fabian & Hamo:

Not much moon tonight, so it's hard to
tell - are these all palmers? One or two

are hiding something - hard to say what.
That fair-faced lad is rich but pretending

to be not-so. T'other fellow next to him
is dangerous in some way. I fear for

someone's soul other than his. He seems
miserable enough for a pilgrim, but he's a

shifty one, no doubt. I heard him say his
name is *Hamo* - a falsehood by the way he

muttered. Looks like this lot might just make
lodgings afore curfew, but off goes Hamo -

he's taking a different path already.

Scouting Mission

Hamo speaks:

Although I've only just entered here, my exit I must find,
for when what's done is done, I cannot roam this city blind.

Avoiding the grumpy guards, I'll tease,
faking the hunting owl with ease,
I'll bring those beggars to their knees!
While Hamo's here, I'll do as I please.

Let's look around this noisy night, and take the scenic route,
befuddle the bumbling curfew crew, and walk quietly underfoot.

Avoiding the grumpy guards, I'll tease,
faking the hunting owl with ease,
I'll bring those beggars to their knees!
While Hamo's here, I'll do as I please.

St Agnes' Lane into Cook Street and then along Cross Cheaping,
finding shadows and hiding places, ever so slowly creeping.

Avoiding the grumpy guards, I'll tease,
faking the hunting owl with ease,
I'll bring those beggars to their knees!
While Hamo's here, I'll do as I please.

Edge past the Cross into Broadgate, stay off the beaten track,
I see the house in Spicer Stoke where I'll make my attack.

Avoiding the grumpy guards, I'll tease,
faking the hunting owl with ease,
I'll bring those beggars to their knees!
While Hamo's here, I'll do as I please.

I see the path to Gosford Gate is straight enough for me,
But just in case, here's Much Park Street, where I can hide unseen!

Avoiding the grumpy guards, I'll tease,
faking the hunting owl with ease,
I'll bring those beggars to their knees!
While Hamo's here, I'll do as I please.

Time to blend with the background now, blurring the edges well,
and switch my cloak to Ailwin's brown so no-one else can tell.

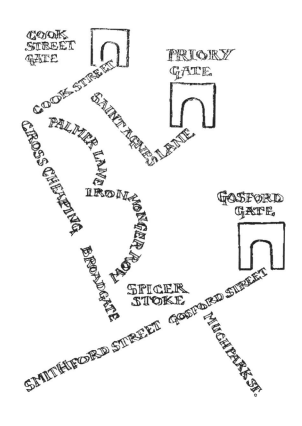

Narrator (Day Has Dawned)

The day has dawned, the curfew's clear,
the pleas of pilgrims fill my ears.

We see the heir among the throng,
as monks say prayers for others' wrongs.

The city's craftsmen toil and sweat -
their day is long, their tasks are set.

As other folk they come and go,
let's listen in to what they know.

The gates will also have their say,
for many stories pass their way.

And who would wish to draw a veil
in lieu of hearing all those tales?

St Osburga's Bones

Fabian speaks:

A restful night to end this week,
the Lord, indeed, my soul did keep.

And shuffling in this pilgrim's line
I'm ever-hopeful of some sign.

Osburga's bones you hold the key -
delay those moving to purgatory.

I pray the Saint and Lord are listening -
father's brow with sweat was glistening,

my home and family he bade forsake,
and begged me to this journey make.

The statues watch in silent stone -
we walk in step and thought alone.

But now I kneel in fervent prayer,
and face the bones with pleading stare,

the smoke and incense in the air,
with candles burning everywhere,
for those we've loved, no longer there.

St Michael's Mason

Robert Stretton speaks:

They say 'twas Botoner that paid
the men with brawn and picks and spade
and now foundations have been laid
we're working to the plans they've made.

Taking our hammers and chisels while bidden,
we'll coax each block to yield what's hidden.

They say 'twas God that moved the man
to make up such ambitious plans
and see these arches, how they span?
For centuries we'll make them stand.

Taking our hammers and chisels while bidden,
we'll coax each block to yield what's hidden.

The rocks are rough and piled up high
and we shall shape them by and by,
and through the years, though they may fly
we'll build a spire to touch the sky.

Taking our hammers and chisels while bidden,
we'll coax each block to yield what's hidden.

And now, 'tis time we had begun
and while we work, we others shun.
We'll bury our secrets in the stone
and build this church until we're done.

Dern Gate

Oh, where will you go Will Crowe, say, where will you go?

Your own Dern Gate darling,
mayhap found someone new
who carries more silver,
whose eyes are true blue.

So where will you go, Will Crowe, oh, where will you go?

I see you must leave here
with your spirit so broken
and a heart that needs mending
after harsh words were spoken.

So where will you go, Will Crowe, oh, where will you go?

'Tis time you were travelling,
for the daylight won't last,
and it may be some hours
before you shall break-fast.

So where will you go, Will Crowe, oh, where will you go?

Mayhap there's a maiden
in some yonder town
awaiting a girdler
to measure her gown.

But where will you go, Will Crowe, oh, where will you go?

Blind Eye

Addy speaks:

We search the bags and sacks,
we watch the crowds and those
with oddly-troubled backs.

We never turn an eye that's blind:
the law's the law, the tax is paid
on everything we ever find.

Folks will try to hide and hutch
and sneak through what might
fill their coffers much.

Sometimes it's in the face or eyes
a sudden look or glance that
tells me I shall find their prize,

or *Time and Tide*, that wretched tune,
a nervous whistle catching like
the madness of the moon.

Ah, here comes Maud, my love,
our friendship strong and true,
blessed, I hope, by God above.

Greyfriars' Gate

Speaking of Dizzy:

I see through Dizzy's play-acting -
the madness in his eyes falls

far short of truth, for the cycles of
the moon plague him not,

nor does the sun's glare confound
him. No, Dizzy's giddy game

brings a beggar's harvest for an
idle planter. But should he

be discovered, then the stocks
will seek him out before

true madness claims him, as
hunger bites and thirst

finally withers his spirit.

Dizzy

I mostly beg by Greyfriars' gate,
touching the timber or
stroking the stone,
but I'm not so simple
when I'm on my own.

My face is fixed with awkward smile,
following pilgrims by the mile.

Weaving through the crowds for a time,
I'll crave a coin with a poor man's rhyme:

Time and tide! we like that song,
you hear it in the market's throng.
Time and tide! we sang along;
that troubadour can sing no wrong!

I notice things but never say,
for too much trouble
would fall my way.

I sleep where I can,
I'm happy alone;
I'm not so simple
when I'm on my own.

Finding The Star

Fabian speaks:

My duty done, I've left the bones as found,
'tis time for me to take a proper look around.

Dusk bestows upon this place a favour,
hiding temptations some pilgrims might savour.

I was told "Go find The Star for the best of ale,
and fine repast." Mayhap I'll hear a merry tale!

After waiting long to see the Saint's remains
'tis time for things that shall a man sustain!

They say The Peacock is the place to stay -
I shall visit on my journey to the Star this day.

The stench is foul and strong in Butcher Row
and I must take pains avoiding any blood that flows!

"Most splendidious is Cross Cheaping's cross" -
no idle boast - before mine eyes all else I see is lost.

The monk's directions: "Into Broadgate, go
then left to Smithford Street and simply follow

thine eyes and nose to Earl Street's place."
The air is heavy and I feel the rain upon my face.

At last I see the bright and busy Star-named inn
and wonder what I shall encounter there within.

Summers' Roses

Jocelin sings:

We gathered fuel and built the fire
the tinder brittle underfoot;
her shrouded body on its trestle,
the priests all murmured as they stood.

But I remembered summers' roses
and the harvests gathered in;
I remembered all her kisses,
each precious moment tethering.

The winter snows had fallen heavy
as had she: first with the chill,
followed swiftly with a fever
fighting for each breath, she stilled.

Yet I remembered summers' roses
and the harvests gathered in;
I remembered all her kisses,
each precious moment tethering.

The children all had gathered round her,
with tears and hearts that would not mend,
holding hands with warm embraces,
watching, waiting for the end.

But I remembered summers' roses
and the harvests gathered in;
I remembered all her kisses,
each precious moment tethering.

I placed a kiss upon her forehead
her skin now pale, bereft of life.
To me her beauty was eternal,
for she had been my loving wife.

Then I remembered summers' roses
and the harvests gathered in;
I remembered all her kisses,
Each precious moment tethering.

As Air Is Light

Though stars be bright, your smile is brighter.
As air is light, your steps are lighter.

Every movement filled with grace,
a blesséd beauty on your face.

I see no others in this room,
for only you dispel my gloom.

And when I heard your joyous laughter,
my heart was lost to me thereafter.

I never heard yon Cupid's bow
but feel his toxin, head to toe.

Oh Bela, Bela, stay awhile,
and let me gaze upon that smile,

or I shall sit like patience must
while all around me gather dust,

watching you with love-struck awe,
a living sculpture, without flaw.

Narrator (Church Bells)

Every church must have its bells
to call its sinners near,

and every sinner must repent
'tis Hell that we all fear.

So, every bell must first be cast
in fiery pits dug deep,

materials, manure and smoke
will make those young boys weep.

The master must procure all this
and off to town he goes,

and we shall see how well he does.
Will Fortune smile? Jove knows!

Buying For the Bell

John De Colsale speaks:

In Corley I have named my price
and we have made a deal.

And now in faith I come to town
to have the bargain sealed.

As master I have shared my skills
and hope I've taught them well.

I let my boys prepare the pit
we need to cast the bell.

But there are things that I must
have from Ironmonger Row,

with wood and rope and beeswax too
before 'tis time to go;

horse manure and straw I've found
on farms along my way,

and maybe with God's blessing
I shall have the best of days!

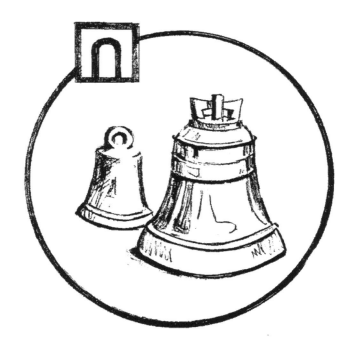

Bishop Gate

(For John de Colsale as he leaves)

A man wanders in to this great city
with a bell to buy for, and afore he

knows it, a tankard of ale later and
he's buying for two bells! Yes, God

and good fortune have smiled on
John de Colsale this fine day! For

Saint Michael's at Stoke was also in
great need of a bell and now they

have a man who shall cast it for
them. Not from these parts - some

say his voice is Nottingham, others
Leicester, but his purse cares not!

The Holy Church and local Prior
shall welcome sinners from here and there
called by bells to repentance and prayer.

ARGENT

The Founding Of Corley Bell

John De Colesale speaks:

I learned a lesson very early in my craft - that
there must be method, but there is no rhythm
in the slow-but-sure work of bell founding.
I dug each casting pit with blistered hands
and built the fires myself - see how all my

apprentices now do the same? I watched my
master many times, and fetched and carried
for him, saw him shape the wood and curl
the rope around it, skilfully creating the core,
observed the way he placed the clay we'd

carried, forming layer on layer, his patience
in action, a mental picture moulded before
the eyes of his participating ever-faithful
boys. Now as master, 'tis my turn to share
the skill, from the argent to the lip, using

the strickle's outline to shape the crown first,
then slipping to the shoulder and inscription
band, but making sure the waist is crafted
carefully - 'tis a fool's approach in taking the
tone of such a bell for granted! The hours

pass before the time comes when the job is
almost done, and I glide and slide my hands
in the skimming of the sound-bow and edging
the lip, setting the moulding wires firmly in
place to live beyond the casting as a reminder

of these moments of mystery and memory afore
the mould is set and ready for lowering into the
pit and the pouring of hot metal, and praying to
Almighty God that he blesses this bell that
will call sinners to his church here in Corley.

Narrator (O'er To the Star)

We're on our way o'er to The Star -
for the town is very busy;

Odo and the Mylner's there,
and I think I've just seen Dizzy!

The son-and-heir has settled in
to keep an eye on Bela,

and Jocelin's busy writing things
that Fabian can tell her!

Bela's playfulness is gone -
her mistress keeps her serving.

Poor Addy's slumber is disturbed -
Maud says he's undeserving!

Other folks have come and gone,
the day is almost done;

the wise are looking weary now,
while young love seeks its fun.

Though one or two are in their cups
are breaking out in song,

our Addy gets to earn his keep
by moving them along!

Odious

Odo speaks:

"Odious Odo", 'tis what they all say
when folks they see me walk their way.

Some make a noise just like they're pigs,
I close my ears – why give a fig?

Most folk leave it at odious, but I don't
care. If it wasn't for *Odo*, 'twould be another

poor soul getting spat on and worse.
I tell 'em to take it up with the churchmen -

they set the fines, I just collect. "Seek
and ye shall find", says the good book,

according to the priests and the bishops,
so that's what I do. Folks hide (or try to),

but I always track 'em down in the end.
I wander beyond the city walls at times,

listening and looking for signs, sneaking
along hedgerows, quiet as a field-mouse.

I wish I had skills and learned a craft. I've
no friends - even Dizzy avoids me.

At least what I do keeps me clothed and fed
and the bailiffs from the door, so spit all

you like, but it isn't me that's judging you -
that's for others and Almighty God to do.

The Mylner

Thomas Hynkley speaks:

Oh, put that down you irksome brat,
and take that off - it's not a hat.

And please don't touch that little chain -
'tis fragile as a drop of rain.

My trinkets tease the finest ladies,
but you can beggar off to Hades!

You have no coin to buy my wares -
leave that alone, go say your prayers!

And do not tip your drinking vessel
near those fine goods upon my trestle!

Mayhap the guards will pass this way
then chains will stop your silly play!

Thomas Hynkley is my name
and I shall find yours out to shame.

Oh, Dizzy, is it? Well we shall see,
for no-one here shall outwit me.

At last he's gone ('tis not a shock.),
mayhap I'll have him in the stocks,

though soon enough my anger fades,
for Dizzy has increased my trade!

Ribbon

Bela to Fabian:

Go buy me a ribbon,
to tie up my hair,

or bring me a trinket
to make people stare,

or buy me some bauble
that sparkles and shines,

or slip me a penny -
I keep all that's mine.

Then wait 'til the candles
have burned themselves out

and I'll meet you outside
there's a curfew to flout.

I know of a place, all quiet and dry,
where time and the night shall both pass us by.

Whisper Me Awake

Fabian & Bela speak:

Whisper me awake my princess,
show me how we'll start the day.

Whisper me awake my sweetheart,
let me wave you on your way.

Whisper me awake my sweeting,
like a gentle summer breeze.

Whisper me awake my honey,
smile like sunlight through the trees.

Whisper me awake my petal,
while the city's watchmen sleep.

Whisper me awake my dearest,
through the city's street's we'll creep.

Whisper me awake my truelove,
let your lips caress my ear,
let me see your radiant beauty,
let me hold your body near.

Cook Street Gate

(For Fabian and Bela)

I watched them kiss, lips brushing
gently and parting in smiles as many

covered wagons headed through to
market from the rutted road, creaking

under the weight, the steam rising
steadily from the beasts of burden.

Bela's innocence is touching. She is
naught but a lowly maid and he is

one who shall inherit. Many false
promises will be made and her heart

will be broken. Had she carried the
horn of plenty, mayhap his bones

would be broken. That's just how it is,
and how it has always been.

The Goldsmith of Spicer Stoke

Richard Burnell speaks:

Goldsmiths guard their precious skills,
but Guilds have rules we must fulfil:

apprentices are hard to keep -
bone-idle lads, or half-asleep!

My precious gold is hidden away,
though thieves may try my locks each day!

I keep the hounds out in the yard -
by day and night its gates are barred.

But I like it here in Spicer Stoke,
serving the ladies and gentle-folk.

The bells of churches mark the time
while jewelled chains I link so fine.

Though there are others in this town,
I think myself the best around.

In filing, forging and casting true,
I craft each bijou, just for you.

Here Again

Eva speaks:

Masci is working upstairs at the loom,
when Odo my brother, walks into this room.

He's out and about noting everyone's sins,
but I cannot forsake him, as he is my kin.

My husband's unhappy he's called here again,
disturbing our labours and bringing us shame.

Poor Odo gets lonely, I know how mud sticks,
but he's chosen his path - only he can fix this.

Masci's now calling, I'll bring him some ale,
I'll say that the pot's on or some other tale.

Then Odo must leave before time takes its toll,
While I say a prayer that God save his soul.

The Weaver's Lot

Masci speaks:

With warp and weft
and skill so deft
we weave and weave.

In darkened rooms
we drive our looms
and weave and weave.

With wash and lye
they bleed the dye
as we weave and weave.

On tenterhooks
they stretch each nook
as we weave and weave.

In fuller's earth
they show their worth
as we weave and weave.

Where you stand there,
like ghosts we were
as we weaved and weaved.

Spon Gate on Sunday

Saint John the Baptist stood here long,
so long before I came;
whatever glory I possess,
his is not the same.

'Tis oddly such a joy each time
to hear the bells so loud,
as Christians flock to hear the Mass
and through this gate they crowd.

Weavers, dyers, walkers call
and amble side by side,
then into church where God sees all -
there is no place to hide.

The smell of incense fills the air
as do the chants and song,
and afterwards a noise erupts
when from the church they throng.

Most folk do stay, but others flee
for they have things to do,
'tis Sunday and with mouths to feed,
so Spon Gate they go through.

We are so close, this church and me,
as brothers built in stone.
Through darkest days and darker nights
we never are alone.

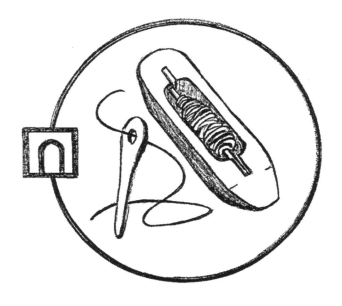

Hill Street Gate

(For Masci)

Masci strides this way, fists clenched and angry
at Eva's brother Odo calling upon her daily for
ale and bread, with tales of his misery and woe.

Masci's love for Eva runs deep, but he insists
they cannot keep feeding Odo in such times.

Weavers work hard, forever at the mercy of
daylight and other masters, so when someone
calls, each precious hour is lost for weaving.

Mayhap other weavers in the city will come
lend an ear and speak to keep him calm - I see

Guild friends John Arowe and William Thomas
accost him now.

Her brother is reviled by all with each so keen to scold.
How different, then is Eva's soul, her beauty to behold.

Love-bond

Maud speaks:

I met my truelove long ago
when I was young and free;
I wasn't much to look at then,
but he always smiled at me.

I made my truelove wait for me,
and patience he did show.
Those days and weeks of secret smiles
just made that love-bond grow.

I caught my truelove's eye one day
when summer's heat was full.
He swept me up in a tide of love,
soft, with the strength of a bull.

But battles called and took him off,
and Bela came along.
For such long years in Coventry,
I've sung that special song.

Time and tide, time and tide,
Addy will never know,
time and tide, time and tide,
How much I missed him so.

Garland

Jocelin sings:

She put a garland on my head,
as the kindling caught the flames;
the sun was burning, sinking low,
then we played midsummer's games.

The wind was whirling on the water
as the ripples rolled away,
and magic's mayhem played its part
as the night replaced the day.

'Twas something in the way she moved,
how she stopped and then stood still;
the voice that sang was pure and true,
to tease and then to thrill.

Heartbeats quickened in the darkness,
an inner clock that marked the time;
under moonlight, shadows dancing,
whispered promises and rhyme.

Then a mist appeared from nowhere,
a sleepiness upon the land;
silent voices, secret glances,
once again, she took my hand.

And when the brightness of the morning
blurred my bleary view that day,
I looked around but she was nowhere -
as dream or truth, she'd paled away.

Little Park Gate

(For someone the worse for wear)

Here is another soul looking lost, as many
do when the light finds them by this gate.

Earl Street and Jordan Well may be bright,
but Much Park Street is darker and a little

misty now. And down here, some say that
'tis eerie by Dead Lane - with superstitious

talk of souls that are restless, all buried here,
died of the plague, walking among the living

after nightfall, but none have passed through
here! Any fool, staggering or upright, found

to be in their cups will catch a curfew's fine
unless they creep like mice towards home.

And while others may eat or sup or sleep or fight,
There's no palliasse for me on this mistiest of nights!

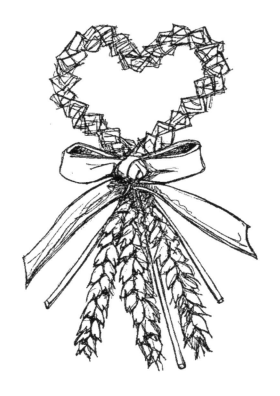

Narrator (Back At The Star)

The Star's the finest place to be
'tis where the ale best flows.

'Tis where the stories intertwine,
their threads will weave it so.

The cappers and the furbishers
are talking by the fire;

the farmer's hoping all his hands
go home before they tire.

The lovers smile as Jocelin sings
another song of love;

Our Maud and Addy look content -
they fit like hand and glove.

Keep The Cappers Happy

Richard Austen speaks to John Essex of the Leet Court:

Keep the cappers happy, John,
we're trying to make our way,
working just as hard as furbishers,
giving thanks for every day.

We all wear caps that fit us, John,
'tis how the world must be -
there's no good being sour-faced,
the way you look at me.

Just ease the murage on us, John,
and let us find our feet,
and keep the cappers sweet awhile,
so please talk to the Leet.

Mayhap the pinners will be asking next
or other crafts as poor,
and but for God's good graces, John
you'd be knocking at this door.

So, keep the cappers happy, John,
we're trying to make our way,
working just as hard as furbishers,
giving thanks for every day.

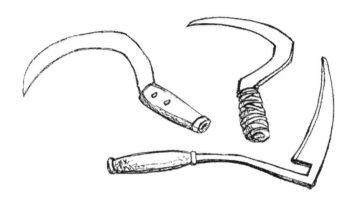

To The Harvest

A farmer at The Star speaks:

Let us finish off our drinking now
and bid our friends good night.

Let us gather in the early morn
to the birdsong of the dawn chorus.

Let us ready ourselves and sing our
songs while the air is fresh and clear.

Let the harvests be gathered in joyfully
while the sun shines above in a blue sky.

Let the earth rest a while before the
ploughing and tilling of the soil begins.

Let the fruits of our labour bring us
much good fortune at the markets.

And when we are done, let Autumn
shed its tears, lamenting at the
passing of another summer.

Farewell

Fabian speaks to Bela:

Oh Bela, my love, my life, my all -
I must away, for family duty calls.

Oh Bela, my love, my world without end,
I must return home and my father attend.

Oh Bela, my love, my life, my all -
I must away, for family duty calls.

But I shall return for your kisses so sweet
and watch you sway on those pretty faerie feet.

Oh Bela, my love, my life, my all -
I must away, for family duty calls.

I shall mourn every minute that we are apart
'tis you, 'tis you that have captured my heart.

Oh Bela, my love, my life, my all -
I must away, for family duty calls.

And I shall come back as soon as time allows
for the tying of knots and the taking of vows.

Oh Bela, my love, my life, my all -
I must away, for family duty calls.

Your eyes are like jewels when seen by candle's light -
I shall think of them often in the darkest of nights.

Oh Bela, my love, my life, my all
I must away, for family duty calls.

Waiting For You

Bela speaks to Fabian:

I will wait for you, watching the tides
rise and fall, scanning the horizon,
looking for signs.

I will wait for you, while the lazy moon
waxes and wanes and I will sleep
lightly, listening for the footsteps of
your approach.

I will wait for you until the frosts of winter are
but a shivering memory and the frozen earth
revives once more in the sunshine of
an advancing spring.

I will wait for you, until summer's heat
gives way to autumn's golden canvas,
when heaven's stars align
and we shall stand side by side,
hand in hand, poised and ready
for the dance of our lives.

Narrator (The Morning After)

The Star lies still and quiet – 'tis very early morn;
young Bela is awake, her ribboned-hair adorned.

Maud sleeps very softly, while Addy's out on guard.
The hungry cat? He pounces, hunting mice out in the yard.

Our slumbering young Jocelin, he dreams of better verse,
or a very wealthy Lady will add coins to his purse.

Poor Odo snores alone while Ailwin sits and plots;
our Dizzy's sipping beggared ale and counting what he's got.

Those dozing craftsmen, townsfolk, all too soon will wake
as heavy carts and wagons a very thunder make

when rumbling through the city and its rarely empty streets
filled with harvest produce, and mayhap with some treats!

The Star at last is stirred, and Maud has finally spoken,
so, Bela dresses quietly and hides her truelove's token,

"Oh, time and tide, time and tide," she begins to sing,
"Now my love has gone away, oh what will this day bring?"

Cheylesmore Gate

(For Fabian)

Fabian's mounted for hunting and hawking -
he's had all his sport now he's leaving.

His duty's done here, he's journeying home,
with the maiden he's smitten still grieving.

With friends of his status, surrounded by dogs,
He rides out to the Forest of Arden,

falconer on hand, and hawk on his arm
while young Bela she tends to her garden.

He'll soon be long gone, gone back to his lands,
gone back to the arms of his mother,

while Bela she weeps like a child on the step,
for her heart shall belong to no other.

A Vengeful Murder

Hamo speaks to Richard Burnell:

I've bided my time and waited long years
remembered the beatings and lost all my fear.

No longer a boy that you whipped at your will,
the knife at my side brings a joy and a thrill.

I see you look puzzled, my face bears no scars -
the gaol where you held me had different bars.

Perhaps if I speak of those tasks gone awry
you shall see why I'm back here, face the truth by and by.

That time when I spilled what was too much to hold -
in front of my truelove you did overly scold.

Those shifts where I worked all the day and the night,
'twas never enough - there was always some slight!

Now your eyes have no sparkle, like a bauble that's cheap,
and soon, like a dog, you shall beg at my feet!

See now who's the master, with the blade as I stand?
I shall take what is mine and you shall die by my hand!

Gosford Gate

(At Hamo / Ailwin's exit)

It's always a relief when the gate closes
at twilight and the bar slides into place.

As night surrounds the walls and a gentle
silence finally falls, I can hear the sweet

Sherbourne's song offering a lullaby for the
city, over-tired from its day's commerce.

Much too far from the sights and sounds
of it all, I hear talk of butchers and smiths,

of poor pin-makers, glovers and bakers,
drapers and dyers, walkers and weavers,

ironmongers and costermongers, cooks
and chandlers, vagrants and vagabonds.

Most are welcome, but some are not. - yon
Ailwin who's just left, a bloodied scar upon

his hand - he says he scraped it in a fall -
we do not want his sort within our walls.

Pale As Death

Maud speaks:

Here comes Odo pale as death,
skin like water, out of breath.

'Tis rare to see him look this way -
The Star is silent while he sways.

Addy, sit him down upon a stool -
don't just stand there like a fool!

Give him air and let him speak
and ale to colour up his cheeks.

Bring some bread and broken meat
and let's hear Odo's troubling feat.

Eye Witness Account

Odo speaks:

Trailing Ailwin to Trinity,
he always failed to notice me.

To Spicer Stoke went striding, he,
just where the goldsmith's house would be.

I saw him leave poor Richard's place,
a worried look upon his face.

With dagger sheathed and bloodied hand
he made his way out as he'd planned.

The goldsmith staggered then and fell,
and soon was dead, as all can tell.

I followed Ailwin through the crowd,
my shouts drowned out by church bells loud.

But he was smart, switched cloaks in flight
and disappeared then out of sight.

I spied his cap, but just too late
as he did flee through Gosford Gate.

Hue and Cry

Addy speaks:

God's blood for that's a sorry tale.
Oh Maud, my love, please bring more ale!

Odo be sure of Ailwin's face -
We must not add to your disgrace.

If this be true then we must act,
and do our duty with these facts.

If truth be found in all you say
then we shall find our man this day!

Time and tide, time and tide,
Let us raise the hue and cry!

Time and tide, time and tide,
we'll catch the culprit by and by!

I'll lead the guards and give him chase –
we'll seek out every hiding place.

He won't get far while we have breath –
he'll pay for Richard's violent death.

Time and tide, time and tide,
Let us raise the hue and cry!

Time and tide, time and tide,
we'll catch the culprit by and by!

Gifts

Jocelin sings:

When she took my hand,
she promised me treasure,
but not for to carry-oh.
Then we lay in the long grass
where the seed-heads did tickle
and the seed-heads did tease,
as we talked of our love
and let the time fly
like the birds to the trees.

Then she offered me more
than a harvest of gold
and a strongbox of silver
as we lay in the long grass,
where the seed-heads did tickle
and the seed-heads did tease,
talking of love, and making our plans,
with the wind in the trees.

When she gave me such gifts as
the stars in her eyes,
and the smile on her lips,
we lay back in the long grass,
where the seed-heads did tickle
and the seed-heads did tease,
talking of love, and whispering our names,
cooled by the breeze.

And I still have that gift of the stars
in her eyes and the smile on her lips,
but 'tis only a memory now,
a dream if you will,
from a time in the long grass,
where the seed-heads did tickle
and the seed-heads did tease,
when talking of love and whispering
our names carried off on the breeze.

Well Street Gate

As Radford Brook goes babbling past
the time near here does not go fast,

A cart or two might stay or linger,
and japes be played with wagging finger.

The guards will grumble all the while,
but heading home is when they'll smile.

By day, 'tis peaceful, soft and still,
we hear the birdsong sweet and shrill.

By night the wheel of Radford Mill
breaks up the quiet and the still.

But time and tide, here's wind for their sails,
for someone's brought the evening's ale!

Time and tide, creep slow like snails,
'Tis time, 'tis time, to end our tale.

Narrator's Epilogue

And, so my friends, the time has come
to leave this tale, though we're not quite done.

Each stone unturned has played its part,
for what lies beneath, our history charts ...

Beneath These Stones

The remembered and forgotten lie
beneath these streets and stones,
in plague-pit or necropolis
in ordered rows of bones.

By Neolithic necromancers,
or high-priests with a cause,
lie sacrificial children
who drew life's shortest straws.

There are Romans here and Vikings,
there are Anglo-Saxons too,
the grave is multicultural -
it's for red blood and for blue.

We have cordwainers and cobblers
who made shoes for many feet,
and vintners drained of finest wines
at last their maker meet.

There are wainwrights with their wheelwrights
who made those wagons roll;
there are millwrights here with millers
where the flour-dust took its toll.

Look for blacksmiths who forged friendships
with ploughwrights and their ploughs,
where the hammer beat the metal
as the sweat dripped from their brows.

Here lie chandlers for whom candles
are no longer lit or burned,
and archers, pike-men, musketeers
when peace again was spurned.

See those brewers who made barrelled ale
offering something safe to drink;
there are scholars and philosophers
with no more cause to think.

Ah, those butchers who killed livestock
and hanged them on the hook;
there are bakers with their kneading hands
and scullery maids and cooks.

Here lie milliners who made hats and more,
their madness hard to stand,
and glovers who sold such fine goods
regardless of the hand.

The tanners rest here free at last
from their caustic tanyard stench,
and whittawers whose saddles shone
after labouring at the bench.

There are weavers who were almost blind
from working in poor light,
near mercers and their profiteers
who thought that this was right.

There'll be fullers here and dyers too
with their tenterhooks in rust;
maybe yeomen guards and others who
once held such jobs of trust.

There are drapers dressed in finest cloth -
each seamstress did them proud.
Town criers rest in silence now,
no need to please the crowds.

There are prostitutes and destitutes,
their plights now long forgotten,
whose lives were short but never sweet,
their lot in life so rotten.

Beneath these stones they lie at rest,
those diggers of graves dug deep -
a dreadful task in plague or worse,
they've more than earned their sleep.

Here lie widows, orphans, husbands, wives
who died rich or oh-so-poor,
they share this earth as common land
as they knock on Heaven's door.

Like pebbles on a shingle beach
where the seaweed makes its slime,
here lie so very many stones
worn by a sea of time.

Author's Notes

Historical Characters

As mentioned at the beginning of the book, the Leet Book was used as a source for most of the non-fictional names. This was a random exercise in a sense, where I just read through it looking for names and events that matched an activity, a place, or just for inspiration. *A Coventry Tale* is set in and around the year 1450, but I have taken some liberties with time-frames in using characters based on real people from the 1400s.

John Arowe was a weaver who lived in Bishop Street, and his name was plucked from a list of those who loaned money to the King in 1451, contributing one shilling and eight pence.

Richard Botoner was at one time a Mayor of Coventry, elected as a new officer of the Leet Court in 1435. The Botoners were an extremely wealthy family and contributed greatly towards the construction of St Michael's church (supposedly £100 a year for over 20 years, which was a huge amount of money in those days).

Richard Burnell was a goldsmith who may or may not have lived in Spicer Stoke, which was primarily a small row of grocer's shops (and dwellings) between Holy Trinity Church and Butcher Row (*spicer* is a medieval term for *grocer*). I really liked the name of the area and couldn't resist placing Richard there. There is a photograph of Spicer Stoke Gate in the Herbert Museum Reference Library in Coventry, most probably taken when redeveloping the city centre after the second world war.

John De Colsale worked with metal and was skilled in the art of bell-founding or -casting. I have again played with the time-frame - he made a church bell for Stoke St. Michael's and one for Corley around 1410.

Will Crowe was a *girdler* (someone who makes belts) who lived on Bayley Lane. The clergy would have been major customers of Will Crowe and his fellow girdlers, as would most people who required something a little smarter to tie around their waist than a piece of old rope! Girdlers were among the poorer craftsmen and struggled to pay their contribution when the *Miracle* (now known as *Mystery*) plays required funding. Will Crowe loaned the King a shilling in 1449.

Richard Austen was a *capper* (a cap-maker) who lived in Spon Street and is first mentioned in the Leet Book in 1435. The cappers first appeared as a guild in Coventry in 1450, and would be subject to the same taxes as the other craftsmen and guilds, so the poem I've written is a plea to the Leet Court to be a little lenient until the cappers were fully established and ready to pay the full amount. Richard Austen joined the Leet Court in 1450, so his poem reflects the kind of conversation that two members of the Court might have had in an inn over a tankard of ale.

There is a John Essex, referred to as a *furbisher* (someone who removes rust from metal), in a 1449/50 Leet Book record regarding the collection of funds to pay for armour for those who would 'preserve the peace within the City of Coventry' and 'strengthen the King's laws'. This may (perhaps) distinguish him from the John Essex in who is mentioned repeatedly in the Leet Book as a jury member and was elected Mayor in 1440 – it is this latter John Essex petitioned by our capper, Richard Austen.

Thomas Hynkley was a *mylner* - someone who sold fancy goods. The etymology of the word is *someone from Milan*, a *Milaner*. Thomas lived in Cross Cheaping and loaned the King one shilling and eight pence in 1449. He sprang to life for me as someone whose goods might fascinate Dizzy on market day.

Robert Stretton was a mason and his name was a good fit with the poem I had in mind; other masons were listed in the Leet Book, but his name just seemed to match the character nicely. Unfortunately, I have not been able to find out where he lived.

William Thomas was another weaver, who loaned money to the King in 1451. He lived in Bishop Street and contributed one shilling and eight pence – the largest amount donated in Bishop Street was over six shillings, the smallest being one shilling.

References

Listed below are some useful references I have used in the writing of *A Coventry Tale*, with individual vignettes of wonder (from this poet's perspective!). Some may only be visible via a reference library, so I have included online references which offer an alternative.

1. *The Coventry Leet Book (or Mayor's Register)*, transcribed and edited by Mary Dormer Harris. Published 1907 by Kegan Paul, Trench, Trübner & Co. Ltd.

2. An Internet Version of *The Coventry Leet Book* can be found by some targeted searching for it at this website: https://archive.org/

3. *The Story of Coventry* by Mary Dormer Harris, published 1911 by J M Dent & Sons Ltd.

4. Internet Version of *The Story of Coventry* can be found by searching for *Mary Dormer Harris* at this website: https://www.gutenberg.org/

5. *Dr Troughton's Sketches of Old Coventry* by Dr Nathaniel Troughton. Publication date unknown, published by B T Batsford (London).

6. *Coventry's Heritage* by Levi Fox, published (second edition) 1957 by The Coventry Evening Telegraph.

7. *The Mystery of The Coventry Cappers* by Peter King, published 2001 by Continuum.

8. *Coventry - Echoes of the Past* by Frank Roden, published 1984 by Coral Productions.

9. *The Little History Of Coventry* by Peter Walters, published 2019 by The History Press.

10. *The Canterbury Tales* by Geoffrey Chaucer, published 1901 by Gay & Bird.

11. *The Wharncliffe Companion To Coventry* by David McGrory, published 2008 by Wharncliffe Books.

12. *The Victoria History Of The County Of Warwick* (Volume VIII) by University Of London Institute Of Historical Research, published 1969 by Oxford University Press.

13. *The Church Bells of Warwickshire* by Rev. H. T. Tilley and H. B. Walters, published 1910 by Cornish Brothers Ltd (Birmingham).

14. Historic Coventry website:
   https://www.historiccoventry.co.uk/main/main.php

15. Medieval Coventry website:
   http://medievalcoventry.co.uk/

ABOUT THE AUTHOR

Paul lives and works in Coventry and has published several poetry collections. He was a poet-in-residence at the *Concealment & Deception* exhibition in Royal Leamington Spa and *Guest Poet* at an event celebrating International Poetry Day. Paul has also been privileged to share his poetry at St John The Baptist Church in Fleet Street, Coventry, within their *Festival of Peace & Reconciliation* for Remembrance Day in November. Paul featured as guest poet at Coventry's Central Library to coincide with the launch of his book *Journey To The Front* in 2018.

Try finding Paul on Facebook under *Paul-AM-Palmer-Poetry*, or on Twitter, or via his blog – the links are below.

http://twitter.com/paulpalmerpoet

http://paulampalmer.wordpress.com

ABOUT THE ILLUSTRATOR

Paul and Steve met while they were students at Coventry Lanchester Polytechnic (now Coventry University). Steve gained a degree in Fine Art, before returning to his native Yorkshire to begin a career as a nurse. Now retired, he enjoys having more time to dabble in art again.

Other Books by Paul A M Palmer:

Boys On The Battlefield – Published by CreateSpace (2015)
ISBN-13: 978- 1511408837

Who Will Carry Me? – Published by CreateSpace (2015)
ISBN-13: 978-1508672920

Shelling Peas – Published by CreateSpace (2015)
ISBN-13: 978-1511499309

Sea Of Hands – Published by CreateSpace (2016)
ISBN-13: 978-1542436526

Watching The Sand – Published by CreateSpace (2017)
ISBN-13: 978-1542436526

Journey To The Front – Published by CreateSpace (2018)
ISBN-13:978-1530278909

Perspective – Published by CreateSpace (2018)
ISBN-13: 978-1979700610

Locked In – Published by Kindle Desktop Publishing (2019)
ISBN-13: 978-1722161224

Printed in Poland
by Amazon Fulfillment
Poland Sp. z o.o., Wrocław